THE GREEDY GOAT

a traditional tale
retold by Faye Bolton

illustrated by Paul Borg

MONDO

This edition first published in the United States of America in 1996
by **MONDO Publishing**
By arrangement with MULTIMEDIA INTERNATIONAL (UK) LTD

Printed in Hong Kong
First Mondo printing, February 1996
00 01 9 8 7 6 5 4

ISBN 1-57255-113-5

Originally published in Australia in 1986 by Horwitz Publications Pty Ltd
Original development by Robert Andersen & Associates and Snowball Educational

One day an old woman was cleaning her house when she found a silver coin.

"My oh my, what shall I buy?" wondered the old woman.

"I know, I will buy a little bit of rice and make myself a nice creamy rice pudding." And that is what she did.

She set the pudding on the table to cool and went outside for some water.

Soon a goat came by and smelled
the rice pudding.

The greedy goat jumped in the window and ate up all of the rice pudding, to the very last grain.

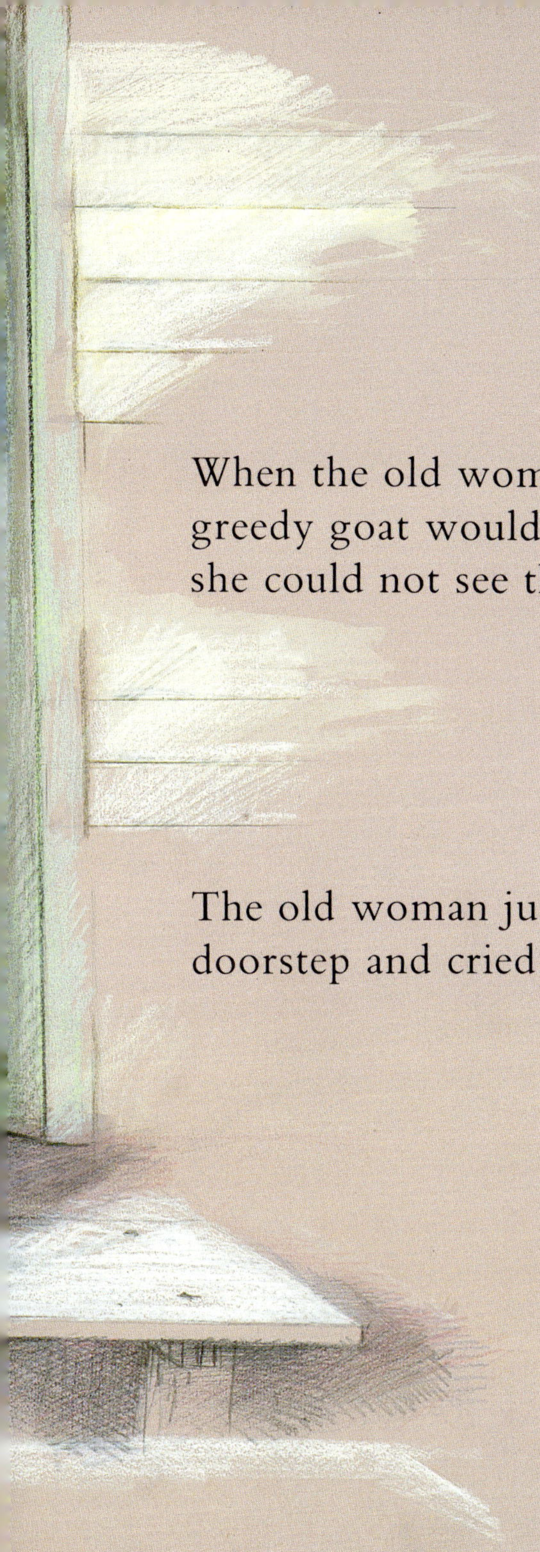

When the old woman returned, the greedy goat would not let her in and she could not see the rice pudding.

The old woman just sat down on her doorstep and cried.

CLOP-CLOP-CLOP. A donkey came by.
"What's wrong old woman?" asked the donkey.
"A goat's in my house and won't let me in," she said.
"Don't worry," said the donkey. "I'll get the goat out."

Knock! Knock!

"Who's there?" bleated the goat.

"It's me!" said the donkey.

"Off with you, I'm a fighting goat.
My two big horns will rip your coat!"

This scared the donkey, and it galloped off down the road.

PAD-PAD-PAD. A dog came by.

"What's wrong old woman?" asked the dog.

"A goat's in my house and won't let me in," she said.

"Don't worry, I'll get the goat out," said the dog.

KNOCK! KNOCK!

"Who's there?" bleated the goat.

"It's me!" said the dog.

"Off with you, I'm a fighting goat.
My two big horns will rip your coat!"

This scared the dog, and it scampered off down the road.

PATTER-PATTER-PATTER. A sheep came by.

"What's wrong old woman?" asked the sheep.

"A goat's in my house and won't let me in," she said.

"Don't worry. I'll get the goat out," said the sheep.

Knock! Knock!

"Who's there?" bleated the goat.
"It's me!" said the sheep.

"Off with you, I'm a fighting goat.
My two big horns will rip your coat!"

This scared the sheep, and it trotted off down the road.

TIPPY-TIPPY TIP. A mouse came by.

"What's wrong old woman?" asked the mouse.

"A goat's in my house and won't let me in," she said.

"Don't worry. I'll get the goat out," said the mouse.

KNOCK! KNOCK!

"Who's there?" bleated the goat.
"It's me!" said the mouse.

"Off with you, I'm a fighting goat.
My two big horns will rip your coat!"

This didn’t scare the mouse away.
“I’m much less than half your size, but I’ve four sharp claws to scratch your eyes.”

This scared the goat, and it rocketed out of the window.

After this, the mouse and the old woman lived happily together to the end of their days.